LATE-STAGE
EVERYTHING

AARON
ANSTETT

Sagging
Meniscus

Many thanks to the editors of the following journals, where some of these poems first appeared:
$, *Apricity Press*, *indefinite space*, *ellipsis*, *Exacting Clam*, *Softblow*, and *Southern Poetry Review*.

Set in Williams Caslon Text with LaTeX.

ISBN: 978-1-952386-44-2 (paperback)
Library of Congress Control Number: 2022947912

Sagging Meniscus Press
Montclair, New Jersey
saggingmeniscus.com

For Lesley

Contents

Why, not even a rustler'd have anything to do
With this branded bum steer world
This pirate flag headlong disaster course vessel

   –Captain Beefheart, "The Host The Ghost The Most Holy-O"

The world began this morning, God-dreamt and full of birds . . .

   —Patrick Kavanagh, "Spring Day"

LATE-STAGE EVERYTHING

Hello!

The universe began
then a bunch of things happened
all at once forever thereafter.
I'm not here to trash-talk existence,
but few movies could not be improved
by chimpanzees in silver fezzes popping wheelies
on mini-bikes around and around the town square.
I thought *illo tempore* meant in a bad mood.
I thought an *idée fixe* fixed broken thinking.
Somewhere in the world a person
enjoys the happiest moment.

Traffic Toward Which We Sleepwalk, Ledge on Which We Drift

What constitutes Anstett's sociohistorical context? A mishmash
of austere grandeur and gaudy terror, the world's music
summoned by finger tap during rise of robots and decline of icecaps.

He's so many data points of purchasing history in late-era capitalism.

Anstett longs to accomplish the impossible, delay the inevitable,
trace back those squiggly, crisscrossing paths of oxygen
molecules we amply sample to create a fluent, useful map.

Let us praise the thisness and thatness of witness, the telling of individual
      particulars.

He watches sunlight move with purpose across the surfaces, reflective
buildings the colors of precious metals and along the sidewalks
favelas of factory pallets, cardboard, tents of blue tarp wind snaps.

While forests smolder, species flicker, he adds his measly figurings to the stack.

Shelter in Place

> "It was evening all afternoon.
> It was snowing and it was going to snow."
> —Wallace Stevens, "Thirteen Ways of Looking at a Blackbird"

It was Monday all week.
It sleeted and it was going to sleet.

It was minute-by-minute all month.
It misted and it was going to mist.

It was February all fall.
It drizzled and it was going to drizzle.

It was indoors all year.
Everything felt elsewhere.

It was in-between all interim.
It lingered and it was going to linger.

It was intermission all through the film.
We were waiting and we were going to wait.

It was lonely all over.
It was dark and it was going to darken.

It was zoom-in high noon all midnight.
It was topsy-turvy and it was going to worsen.

It was ennui all season.
It was boring and it was going to bore.

It was maelstroms all doldrum.
It unnerved and unnerved.

It was distance all directions.
It dizzied and it was going to dizzy.

It felt normal all at once.
It was happening and it was going to happen.

It was often all we could do.

Whatever Killed the Dinosaurs

Then my nation failed to agree on ass vs. elbow vs. hole in the ground.
Then all manner of reality mimicked implausible plots.
Still, even the most depraved among us yearned purely,

longed, for example, to build a machine that runs
naked like sudsy Archimedes yelling "Eureka" through the streets.
In childhood the rusty mesh of screen windows smelled

like rain and old pennies. Let's stay the right amount of stupid
to consider it a miracle objects persist. With spikes and ridges,
hostile architecture benches prevent the unhoused from resting.

A civilization's emblem remains how it treats its wounded,
its hounded, sooty outdoor denizens, open-air residents.
In flurries and skirmishes litter goes to-ing and fro-ing.

The invisible strings between things tremble and tangle.
Under the sky's *ancien regime*, let us catalog sorrows,
gleaming antiquities, in self-portrait as whatever killed the dinosaurs

depict ourselves as leading theories: sunlight-obscuring clouds
of volcanic ash or asteroid collision, then ask a credentialed, faraway
face in rectangle for multisyllabic pharmaceuticals to make it all bearable.

May Day

"Let the millionaire go naked, stark naked!"
—César Vallejo

May the multi-billionaires bankrolling proxy cock rockets for the 1% to escape stop.

May they instead fund food desert grocery stores, wellness checks, dental exams, universal health care, apprenticeships, journalists, trade school, college, trains, buses, marching bands, drumlines, symphonies, poetry readings, and neighborhood puppet shows, two free cold drinks per attendee.

May solar panel and wind turbine farms replace golf courses and parking lots.

May megachurches, shopping malls, and munitions factories shelter the shelterless.

May corporations and the rich pay their taxes like any entry-level janitor.

May minimum income let no one hunger.

May guns become curios.

May not one more child be shot.

May all go garmented as wanted.

May no one struggle between lights or groceries, groceries or medicine, medicine or rent.

May throwing money at problems solve them.

Unlimited music streaming services, tiny homes, and spicy vegan snacks for everyone!

My brain's a pessimist, my heart a Marxist, stomach an anarchist, feet the downtrodden.

My soul's on the side of kids throwing rocks at cops.

May only their helmets and shields be thumped.

May anyone ill be healed.

May the North Atlantic garbage patch—marine debris and microplastics hundreds of miles across—be engineered to serve as refuge paradise for everyone whose islands rising waters overwhelm.

May personal solar-powered cooling suits be distributed to the populace, embroidered with one of three slogans in Esperanto: "Hot and bothered," "Just chilling," and "Sorry."

May hands exert themselves for common purpose.

May the sleep of the people be bountiful.

May the dreams of those sleeping in work clothes contain no labor.

May we wake with the happy idea of infinite wishes.

The Debatable Immutable

Our narrator in an early sentence reckons
the soul's escape velocity by extrapolating
from energy outputs of dam's collapse.
The baby's first curriculum: anatomy and physics.
Genesis it's a wonder anything got done,
all that begatting. When the universe expands
beyond recognition with what material refurbish it?
Glisten of grain sack mice and weather ransack?

Hello, I tell my brain, *you big dummy, think*!
Of vittles sizzling in skillets let us offer all thanks.
When the aliens appear, I believe they'll materialize
as mysterious aromas or waves in the atmosphere.
Until then, Lord, please
keep stitched these umpteen smithereens.

Jot and Whit

Fray of the fabric in timeframe's lapses
sends tangles of ellipses skittering scatterplot,
atoms fetching atoms, mulishly minuscule.
In the pharmacy of writing, poetry's toxin

and medicine. Pristine antique paper outfoxed
elements. Nature remains the greatest antagonist.
From lines in the panhandler's bare palm
number the days now to apocalypse.

Along the body's interiors, inimitable scribbles.
Through smoke-soaked air, the rust-color sunset.
When the world ought to make me persona non grata,
I like watching a muted choir to see

many mouths shaping themselves the same way.
Afternoon arrives airy and ethereal as hearsay.
I heed and ignore my brain chemicals' mixed signals.
I like best exactish measurements, your morsel, your smidgen.

One History

I was born during a riot and I haven't slept well since.
Let's call the tawdriness of history a sequence of events.
Eventually all eventualities commence.
In everything an aftermath, everywhere bears prints.
Someone tell me who said, "There are whispers, there are hints."
Like a back road's buckshot sign the moon looks full of dents.
Which people believed stars light where fabric rents?
I recall the sloshing Pacific blue of innumerable tints.
Two objects inhabiting same space? Collision and coincidence.
Existence seems a series of happy and unhappy accidents.
If only a word like *bread* were what it represents.
To live well or poorly extracts a great expense.
The uprising was put down by national defense
using truncheons, prods, and other instruments.

Help, Predictive Text, Help Me

In this picture I look like an idiot
wishing things otherwise or stick
figure visionary imagining traffic
island shelters for the unhoused
who on them ply oranges,
newspapers, pleas on cardboard.

I will never write a long poem
historicizing a river nor sestina
whose every end word's "and,"
envoi and all, but many elective
surgeries when I win the lottery
at long last grant me the face
of a rich and happy man.

When I'm Ghost, Floaty, Outline

ill-defined, all my outlandish
specifics exactish, I'll moan

"Enh" and "Enh" and "Enh"
again and mean it if you ask me

how I like the afterlife and/or
to haunt the house no more.

Through thread-bare air I'll drift
spectral—get this—present

absence intent on useful mischief:
wiping crumbs from counters,

cleaning windows, polishing
whatever precious metal

you possess to such a luster
my fuzzy reflection unnerves me.

Track the Movement and Charge of a Particle

Imagine a planet with everyone
receiving what they need. Oodles

of hallelujahs already whisper,
abstract and ideal as grammar.

Preserve around me blur
of sudden showers, lightning

strike from every angle. Beauty
and Justice wrestle, tussle, call truce.

I had in mind a kind of motion—drifting
and plunging—energies swapping around.

Under the Swervy Influence

The weather is in love with itself,
attempting poignancy by gimmick.

How uncommunicative the dead, who endured
weather vivid as any.

Military history's crime
reenactment, with kids.

Some say God cannot possibly
oversee alleyway

among the shivering
and wiring of appliances,

God, to whom we may may appear
like flecks in liquid.

Ether Infused with Pursuit

Let us lattice a scaffold—
starfish and honeycomb—
the five-petaled flowers
of human extremities.

Under the swervy influence
of verses, not commodities'
logics, let us valorize
the subliminal verbal,

orality's getaway vehicle.
What a lark to grow distant
and gesture to the flock,
a see-you to the milieu.

Quarterly Report

✳

The messages we expected failed to appear.

As some longed for a color to echo,
foreign powers weaponized the voluble gullible.

In sleep the phrase "lollygag sonnets" repeated.

I formally request a reply
from The Office of Impossible Happenstance
and world map shimmering with the glint
of sunlight on smashed bottles in ditch.

✳

May all particles and forms align
themselves in alphanumerish order.

Neighbors lightheadedly alert one another.

Thank you, Von Quaglio, who first added
mercaptan to scentless natural gas
to imbue it with a startling odor.

✳

From one idea
a musculature
emerges, strung
with nervous
system and various
purposes.

Hands began
to grab branches.

✳

Who believes the skin
an archive of scars?

The past and its structures
disappeared to dust
and ash and mist?

Eels wriggle great distances
from rivers, streams, and creeks
back to the Sargasso Sea, eyes
and fins growing as they swim.

✳

I'm calling the new book
Late-Stage Everything.

As aforementioned, I like best
exactish measurements, your
soupçon, your smidgen, your little bit.

Things that sound more fun
abstract than actual: fiasco, imbroglio, criminal mischief.

We're equally susceptible to the universe's tactics.

For the coming apocalypstacation
pack sufficient ammo and snacks.

We'll survive with gumption,
know-how, homebrew, shotguns.

✳

No responsible medical professional
attaches a prehensile tentacle

to a man's head to distract
from bald spot. But I want it

all and soon: Dead friends
breathing again, food

for every hunger, prosthetic arms
but real fingers, to have whatever

kills me kill me quick, lickety-split, swift
as current through water, flick of wrist.

Among the Calamitous Forces

Windfall fruits

blur, smear.

Seas repeat.

Corrugated

metal structures

tick and snap in sun.

Word cloud of all

help me

ignore conundrums

facts we cannot fix,

icky specifics.

The horse bent

to drink from puddle

in sketch and actual

looks allegorical

but what of?

Rain copies faces,

covering them.

I will tell you

what the TV told me:

Buy these items.

When my soul moves,

body's emigree,

                    I'll hear a product

jingle repeatedly,

                    see behind eyelids

scroll of disclaimer

                    statements, asemic script.

Which pill to stop it?

                    No inscription

most of history.

                    Now reckoning

of least click.

                    No technology

improves

                    upon the mirror.

Or Else

My fellow Americans
go crazy
on camera in public

parks, retail establishments,
yell *Make
my sandwich*, demand

to see the manager,
insist
I am not subject

to your jurisdiction
and *Show
me the law.*

They demolish product
displays,
refuse to leave the premises.

They command *Do
your
own research*,

shout *I fall
under
common law*

and *Your masks will not
do
anything*. It looks fun.

I'd like to scream
whatever
I'm thinking and scatter

merchandise. I'd like to batter
plate glass
with my shoulders.

I'd like to use a baseball bat
and shatter
windshield after windshield

across the parking lots
of America
and make my angers plain.

I'd like to tell your numbskull,
dumbass
relatives and mine a thing

or 6,608,913
and counting.
I'd love to stamp my feet

in cemetery dirt, inform
the dead
and God you're not

the boss of me. I
throw my
little tantrum here

instead, where
few
will see.

Hey, Peter! I Can See Your House from Here!

I joke about Jesus.
I hope he forgives me.

I believe Jesus, no joke,
meant what he said

when he said what he said
about the rich and the poor.

When Jesus claimed
the kingdom of heaven

at hand I believe
he meant literally,

here, now,
if only the plenty

were evenly
issued. Funniest

Jesus joke?
Maybe the one that ends

"Father?"
"Pinnochio?"

Jesus's funniest joke?
Not wine into water

nor reducing multiple
loaves to one, not

the "upon this rock"
pun on Peter's name

but the raising
of Lazarus,

four days dead, over
Martha's objection,

"by this time he stinketh."
Also, upending money

changers' tables
and whipping them. Funny

sense of humor, that Jesus,
who said, "Blessed

are ye that weep now:
for ye shall laugh."

In Manila Envelope from the Truth or Consequences VA

This was found—thought
you might want it back
read the unsigned note
with my father's wristwatch.

Quarterly Report

✳

Every day God prays
furiously
here at the end
of human endeavor

In the archive of what
it sounded like before
you can hear animals

Listen

✳

Tune into the frequency
at which ghosts think.
Release transcripts.
Earth needs answers.

❋

How a many-limbed wriggler
catapults to flutter by God knows
who every day endures a fury.
Soon the zoo may house only holograms.
The vicinity's prevailing weather weirdens
everything. I helped the environment
by buying a great big plastic compost tumbler.
Which of the world's vivid and dingy specifics
fixes attention next who'd guess?

✳

In the future it's one hundred
and hell degrees. Apologies.
News anchors with their faces
blank recite atrocities between
commercials. Imagine the highest
temperature recorded on earth
the new average then scooch the AC a smidge.
Recreationally misusing pharmaceuticals,
maybe I flap my lips about improbably
minuscule camels striding through eyes
of needles. As usual I survive pretending
what is happening is not happening.

✳

Just look what we did with our thumbs
and big ideas: killed everything.
But happy the memory of dumpling
shop on a day so cold one shivers
recalling it, neck wet with snow.
When the call centers and AI conspire
to sell me these goods and services
I'm a smidgen closer to apotheosis.
Where on the world map tattooed
on my torso inscribe *Hic sunt dracones*?

Program

Laughing, speaking, and singing emit an invisible
mist of droplets. The clouds hang like viral veils
that drift and transmit.

I'm punching and kicking the air and winning!

Who convalesces now under an overpass?
Who believes a footprint- and mud-stained
fast food receipt a nation's founding document?

Each new space I inhabit seems text into which I introduce errors.

Asked to describe how architecture sounds, why
does my poor brain imagine not cathedrals
but structures of sheet metal that clang and tick?

Babies keep arriving, naturally operatic.

Tonight the role of sky will be played by smoke,
the role of earth by dust,
the role of water by parts per million.

Voter Fraud Reports

ON ELECTION DAY I CAST MY VOTE
FOR MR. TRUMP AND THEN NEEDED
THE RESTROOM SOMETHING AWFUL
BUT I COULD NOT USE THE FACILITIES
THE TOILET WAS OVERFLOWING IT
LOOKED LIKE HUNDREDS OF BALLOTS
HAD BEEN FLUSHED OR TRIED TO
BE FLUSHED JUST SHAMEFUL THEY
CANNOT FLUSH OUR DEMOCRACY

I personally witnessed the magician
David Copperfield levitate, spin,
then disappear an entire polling place
in a Republican stronghold. Tell Mr.
Giuliani I know I can pick Mr.
Copperfield out of a lineup
and I'm willing to testify in court
so long as it isn't when my shows
are on because the TIVO is broken.
I am praying for Mr. Trump.

Globalist financier and "rich man"
George Soros was handing out $100
bills and asking people to switch
their votes to Biden. Attached
please find a photo of Zero Mostel
in the role of Tevya, on Broadway,
not in the movie. The likeness is striking!

The ghosts of Karl Marx,
Mao Zedong, and Fidel
Castro used Communist
ectoplasm to erase Rep-
ublican ballots at my local
polling place. Then they
scared everyone, murmuring
"Boooo" in German, Chinese,
and Spanish. Here, we talk American!

Some bad men used mind control powers
to sway my vote. Please stop them!

As I filled in the bubble
for Mr. Trump, a spectral
airhorn sounded, startled me,
and made me scribble *Satan,*
Satan, Satan, spoiling my ballot.

545 migrant children separated
from their parents cast ballots
for president. You can bet
any money (dollars, pesos, rubles)
they did not vote for Mr. Trump.
This is fraud because: Most
of them do not know English. None
of them are old enough to vote, some
of them too young to read, some
of them too young to speak.

Newly dead Americans thronged the polls
to cast their votes in hundreds and thousands
from spare rooms and hospital beds nursing
homes VA wards they rose to go petition
the government for redress we could barely move
they crowded the halls in numbers so many

You Again

You were you but not you,
you know, like in dreams,
or the infinite repetitions
on which two mirrors
facing each other insist.
Pillows await lucky
and cement less-lucky heads.
Bodies auger all manner
of onslaught, respite, beds.
Like me I imagine you glad
regardless in whatever conditions—
sunlight, snowstorms—
happy to be there, feeling it
an honor just to be considered.

Until All the Otherwise We Wish

Sooner ask a taxidermied animal—
hide stretched on armature, eyes
polymer resin, posed in lifelike manner—
"What happened?" as demand the particles
of atoms, obstinately toddler animate,
hold still. Why ask how the gods respond
to hosannas and uvula-quivering hallelujahs?

Aspens tremble in a meadow, one
being's tendrils, ringed by colossal
rubble. Replacement molecules
and cells align in a body's particular
patterns, even tattoos of scripture and/or
chimera, impossible, mashup animals.

Jitter and Click Intrinsic to the Circuit

What leaves an inscription at the point of injection
signed *The Troubling Diagnosis*?
What spray-paints undying declarations
on water towers above bereft locales
signed *The Human Face in Photograph,*
Expression Forever in Extremis?

Depicted on antique pottery, hovering
above a dead man's gold-flecked head,
flitting insect the soul makes manifest.

No amount of reasoning deciphers rain
signed *The Distant Vistas,*
signed *Decaying Whispers,*
signed *The Shadowy Saboteur.*

The Universe and Other Ephemera

Generalissimo Muerte soldiers on.

Eerie images of fish, ink-dipped
flesh pressed to rice paper
to record trophy catches,
suddenly seem the saddest thing

I want tattooed all over me.

My New Tattoo

My Venus of Willendorf tattoo
My circle of circles tattoo
My alphabet in every written language tattoo
My bullet and target tattoo
My arrow and stag tattoo
My paired entry and exit wound tattoo
My sunlight through window tattoo
My everything interpenetrates everything tattoo
My unseen forces at play tattoo
My invisibility or gift of flight tattoo
My coffee two sugars tattoo
My first cigarette of the day tattoo
My forklift prongs puncturing shipping container tattoo
My three hours' sleep tattoo
My icicles hanging from beard after walk through Central Park in February
    tattoo
My one-dollar dumplings on Mott Street tattoo
My driving the speed limit now that I'm old and relishing angering other
    drivers tattoo
My less than an inch slack between front and rear bumpers on a hill in North
    Beach tattoo
My I'd love to demolish a house with a 10-lb. hammer wallboard giving way
    like fork through cake tattoo
My shiver in the nerves tattoo
My chewing tinfoil tattoo
My who wouldn't rather be a salamander tattoo
My the system is rigged tattoo
My overthrow the government through general strike tattoo
My satellites hover above us beaming down porn tattoo
My how many dick pics in transmission every millisecond tattoo
My vague longing for antiquity's graffiti tattoo
My desire to disgrace myself globally via all media tattoo
My snail riding a turtle's back and saying *Whee* tattoo
My I scarred this thumb with the other thumb's uncut nail while opening a
    prescription bottle tattoo
My cannot read the label without glasses tattoo
My angels appearing as hovering radiant isosceles triangles tattoo

My waterspout migrating across the shore like the first land animals
          transforming to tornado dervishing around the resort tattoo
My ill-equipped man dragged around by that pauper's purse his belly tattoo
My coils of fog hovering over the Perfume River tattoo
My 10,000 Americans die of the placebo effect each year tattoo

Ex Cathedra All the Live-Long Day

Enthroned, bath-robed in imagined
sanctum sanctorum, I steeple
my fingers and pronounce
stoic Latin maxims ineptly. Mostly
they exhort to brace ourselves
for the body's built-in obsolescence,
its time-release indignities.

Be glad at least once an isolated
drop of rain, all surface and interior,
magnified the full moon's flecked panache.

Let God or whatever iffiness
rush between hearts. *Abstruse*
should be the color and/or name of a flower
whose innards I inhabit, occupied
by prolonged, inconclusive
thinking about a matter.

Quarterly Report

✳

Should you prefer language with texture
and crackle, ample examples
exist elsewhere. To all
the animals I ate I apologize,
but you were delicious
in soups and on sandwiches.
You made me cry,
smoked and spiced and smothered
in sauces. To the humans
doing the dirty, dangerous work,
thank you. I'm sorry. I didn't know.
I thought the moon made it dark
and small people sang in the radio.

✳

A skillet swiftly
to the back of a skull
solves many epistemological questions.
While the circulation of commodities
maps needs and wants, clouds
of colorful smoke imprint
themselves on digital film.
At red lights in rain I stop
the wipers to watch drops
smear and abstract my surroundings.

✳

"Oof" I wish more songs began
or "Wow," exactly apt
responses to the iconic
image called "Earthrise,"
one example, or any morning's
news. "Och" is Scots for "oy,"
expressing regret or surprise.
I recalled reading an unbearably
sad novel I greatly enjoyed,
like life, like life, like life, like life.
Oof. Wow. Och. Oy.

✳

I thought athwart the throat
a thought got thwarted
like eyes in thorns. I thought
the unsaid stuck in craws.
I thought the caws of crows
across the air were weather's cause.
Of course a curse occurs, plural.
Blessings, too, case by case.
On these bases arise cross-purposes.
I thought I felt a nudge from unseen forces.

*

When a punch connects
the head and hand
what happens
if we subtract intent
from action, subject
the object of attention
to clinical standards
ouch it hurts
the facts of the matter
admit my feelings
will not be factored
in the final tally

✳

Time-lapse the continent's palimpsest
of glaciers and invaders.

Lovely and strange, the wobble
and tilt of Brendan Behan singing
"Home, home on the range."

When Johnny Cash sings about Jesus, he means it.

One day soon I fear I'll sway
before the Lord, cowardly hearted,
looking dumb as hell in T-shirt that says
"I'm with stupid" or asks "Who farted?"

This Particular Condition

Causes one to see all things as rapidly
sketched as courtroom artist renderings.

Let's saddle the landscape
with billboards depicting drifting

clouds and/or scenery
they obscure. I'm filthy rich

with terrible ideas and insist
a good, all-purpose declaration

to signify anything, distress
to exaltation, remains "Endless dilemma!"

Heal Thyself

Our new DIY home surgery kit,
Suture Self™, equips you—
the budget-conscious consumer—
to doctor what ails you
at home and on the go.
Have insurance? Bill directly
and avoid the middleman.
Convenient! Educational! Painless!*

* Administer anesthetic sparingly.

On *New Grass* Albert Ayler's Saxophone Sounds

Like the voice

Like the voice of some

Like the voice of some wounded

Like the voice of some wounded animal

Like the voice of some wounded animal god

Like the voice of some wounded animal god loves

Like the voice of some wounded animal god loves sounds

Like the voice of some wounded animal god loves

Like the voice of some wounded animal god

Like the voice of some wounded animal

Like the voice of some wounded

Like the voice of some

Like the voice

The Vocals of Rose Marie McCoy on "Everybody's Movin'" from Albert Ayler's *New Grass* Sound

Terrified, like a lynching
just happened, asking

after the cause of so much migration
sweeping the nation

What could it be, what
could it be?

As Much As I Like How Albert Ayler's *New Grass* Sounds

The quiet after
also I love.

Don't Say "Gay" in Florida, Don't Say "War" in Russia

why we have more guns
than people and people
means everyone babies
prisoners the comatose
in America Lord knows
we love guns more than
anyone born look at
the poor Jesus
said we should sell
everything to feed
and said a lot of things
but not blah blah blah
blam blam blam blam
nor a word about what
we do with whom Christ
guns don't kill people people
who really really like guns do

Small Song

The skeleton inside me yearns
to lounge and lope at liberty.
Aims are what these lines concern.
All the blood the veins contain
evaporates eventually
then falls to earth as snow and rain,
the very blessed earth to which
the body and the bones return.

Sakura Bloom Earlier

Cherry blossoms in Kyoto
peaked this season
the earliest in 800 years

Using the diaries of emperors,
governors, monks, researchers
compiled historical data

Unusual weather fluctuations
cause the cherry trees
to bloom more quickly

In addition to greenhouse gases
the team cites other factors
such as solar and lunar influences

The blossoms signify
impermanence,
a central motif

Their color?
Skin of palm,
tongue's tip.

Scent?
Light, scant,
barely detectable.

Kimono-clad women
take selfies
among blooming blossoms

A motorist stops a vehicle
to take a picture
under a canopy

How many, many things
they call to mind,
these cherry-blossoms!

What a Poem

Is every poem
a conceptual poem
if you think about it?

Is any poem
a visual poem
when seen?

Is an academic poem
a spoken-word poem
when read aloud?

Is a spoken-word poem
an academic poem
if it teaches?

Is a narrative poem
a lyric poem
when it sings?

Is a lyric poem
a narrative poem
if something happens?

Is an experimental poem
not an experimental poem
when it fails?

Is a formal poem
a free-form poem
on a job interview?

Is a difficult poem
an accessible poem
made by someone difficult?

Is an accessible poem
a difficult poem
you understand?

Is a haiku
17/140th
of a sonnet?

Is a list poem
the easiest poem
to "write"?

Is the finish of the poem
shiny as a poem
can be?

What a Poem Does

all day
is wait
for anyone

some you
to say
its share

and do
things
to

Poetry Trailers

In the trailer for this poem, evanescent feelings
bubble within the speaker, if not the reader, like gas in water.

In the trailer for this poem, in a world
on the verge of collapse, a hero triumphs at last.

In the trailer for this poem—filmed in car commercial
landscape sunset crayons—weather grandly happens.

In the trailer for this poem, CGI
zombie aliens fight sexpot CGI phantoms.

In the trailer for this poem,
revenge will be exacted.

The Title of the Poem Is

trap door

    /

        welcome mat

window shade

    /

        eyelid

escape clause

    /

        contract

billboard

    /

        fine print

word

    /

        deed

just as promised

    /

        bait-and-switch

chicken

    /

        fish

open hand

    /

        raised fist

cellar door

    /

        pot lid

everlasting

    /

        blink-and-miss

horizon-wide

    /

        plummet-thin

interruption

    /

        abrupt ahem

a kind of heaven

       /

               fair warning

scratch

       /

               itch

sometimes bold

       /

               sometimes italics

The Title of the Poem Is

drifting toward you,
smoke from igloo,
steam from sauna

it ascends like prayer,
warm air

small flying craft
expel oily smoke
creating writing

visible from land

The Title of the Poem Is

the last thing we need
worry about now

what with many
doldrums and cataclysms

like paintings poems
once lacked titles

preceded in print
by the word

incipit
meaning *it begins*

Democratic Experiment

Any big box store where men patrol
aquaria of jerky, salsa amphora,
weapons Army green, cammo tan,
hunter orange, to be seen, warn,
slung along sweat-panted/gym-
shorted hipbones, display holstered
neon sex toy, shiny, nubbed, running
hard. Confronted, remove ear buds,
listen, nod, say, "It's OK! It's a gun!"

Quarterly Report

✳

One watches the sea repeating.
Historical markers narrate
one version of events.
One country bombed another
and I could do nothing
decades on end.
One time you said
times like these time goes
like songs or poems.
That blood dispersed in filaments
and lightning-tinseled woods
look beautiful means the beautiful
means no one any good.

✳

Exclamations rise from hammered thumb
and toothache, skinned knuckle, snapped shoelace,
accident of birthplace and first language,
ticklish inkling of needing to say something.
Everyone breathes. Everyone sneezes. Everyone
feels awful sometimes and then a little better,
then wonderful, as if the feeling will last forever.

✳

In scripta continua of existence
what puncta what interval where
in infinite scroll of actual here
to there *finisterre* ceaseless
scribble to prolix anonymous

✳

An utterance iterates.

A sentence ends
and opens again.

The world's surfaces
bear wear patterns
and other indicia.

The oldest story
is the Lord
giveth and taketh.

Remember birds,
their calls and wingspans,
air they occupied
the proper vehicle?

90,000 police cameras
watch the streets of Singapore.

A rain makes stones
and little leaves jump.

※

Photo by Lesley Ginsberg

Aaron Anstett has received the Nebraska Book Award, the Backwaters Press Prize, and the Balcones Poetry Prize, among other honors, and has served as a regional poet laureate, instituting a continuing project that places the work of local writers in waiting areas. He works as a technical writer and editor and lives in Colorado with his wife, Lesley.

www.ingramcontent.com/pod-product-compliance
Lightning Source LLC
Chambersburg PA
CBHW020214090426
42734CB00008B/1060